STEP INTO HISTORY

SIEGE!

Can You Capture a Castle?

By Julia Bruce

Illustrated by Peter Dennis

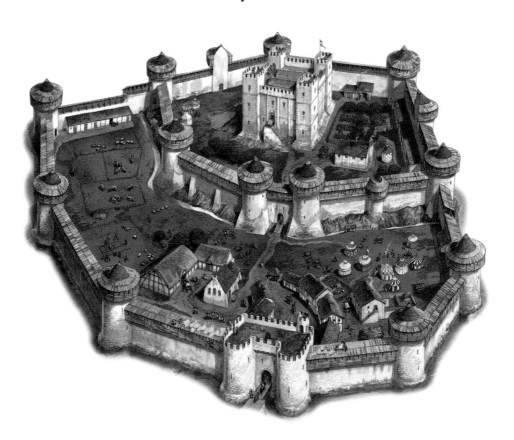

Enslow Elementary

an imprint of

Enslow Publishers, Inc.

40 Industrial Road
Box 398
Berkeley Heights, NJ 07922
USA

http://www.enslow.com

Enslow Elementary, an imprint of Enslow Publishers, Inc.
Enslow Elementary® is a registered trademark of Enslow Publishers, Inc.

US edition published in 2009 by Enslow Publishers, Inc.
First published in 2007 by Orpheus Books Ltd.,
6 Church Green, Witney, Oxfordshire, OX28 4AW, England

Created and produced by
Julia Bruce, Rachel Coombs, Nicholas Harris, Sarah Hartley, and Erica Simms, Orpheus Books Ltd.
Text Julia Bruce
Illustrated by Peter Dennis *(Linda Rogers Associates)*
Consultant Philip Wilkinson

Library of Congress Cataloging-in-Publication Data
Bruce, Julia.
    Siege! can you capture a castle? / Julia Bruce.
        p. cm. — (Step into history)
    Includes bibliographical references and index.
    Summary: "Find out how to successfully plan and lay siege to a castle to defeat the enemy" —
Provided by publisher.
    ISBN-13: 978-0-7660-3475-4
    ISBN-10: 0-7660-3475-5
    1. Siege warfare—History—Juvenile literature. 2. Castles—Juvenile literature.
I. Title
UG444.B87 2008
355.4'4—dc22

                                                        2008020603

To Our Readers: We have done our best to make sure all Internet Addresses in this book were
active and appropriate when we went to press. However, the author and the publisher have no
control over and assume no liability for the material available on those Internet sites or on other
Web sites they may link to. Any comments or suggestions can be sent by e-mail to
comments@enslow.com or to the address on the back cover.

Printed and bound in China.

10 9 8 7 6 5 4 3 2 1

Contents

The Challenge.................4

Planning the Attack...........6

Before the Siege...............8

The Soldiers and
Their Weapons.................10

Setting Up Camp..............12

Castle Defenses................14

The Siege Weapons..........16

The Siege Is Underway....18

Surviving the Siege...........20

How to Undermine
a Tower.............................22

Taking the Castle..............24

Timeline...........................26

Glossary...........................28

Further Reading................30

Index................................31

The Challenge

The year is 1300 and times are troubled. Some powerful nobles have challenged the king for his throne. War is likely. The king has called upon you, his most loyal troop commander, to put down the rebellion. Your number one target is the leader of the nobles, a rebel lord who lives in a new, strongly defended castle.

Your challenge is to capture the rebel lord. If possible, it would be best to do this without a costly battle. You could listen to the rebel lord's complaints against the king and maybe reach an agreement. But if this plan fails, the king has given you permission to besiege the castle. This means preventing anyone from entering or leaving the castle. You can then either starve the castle-dwellers to make them surrender, or take control of the castle by force.

A medieval castle's main purpose is to protect a lord and his family from attack by his enemies. The castle is built like a fortress. It has thick stone walls and is surrounded by a water-filled moat. This is crossed by a drawbridge that can be raised when attackers approach. Also living within the castle walls are the lord's guards, his domestic servants and cooks, knights and their pages and squires, blacksmiths, carpenters, grooms, and priests. The lord himself lives in the keep, a large building inside the castle walls.

If you can make the rebel lord surrender, you will be richly rewarded. You might even receive some of the rebel lord's property. But the task won't be easy. The rebel lord is very ambitious—he would like to be king himself one day. His castle is strongly fortified. A garrison, which is a large group of well-trained soldiers, guards the castle day and night. The lord's castle is designed to endure a siege that may last weeks or even months. However, with the right knowledge and careful planning, the castle can be taken.

There are many things to know when planning a castle siege. What is the best way to break into the castle walls? What soldiers and weapons does a commander have available to him? Can spies be used to help find out about the castle's defenses? Find out the answers to these questions and much more as you go through the campaign step-by-step. Can you help the king successfully capture the castle and regain power?

Planning the Attack

The castle is very strong with many different kinds of defenses. It is on an island with water all around it. This defense is called a moat. You will have to find a way to cross the moat to get to the castle walls. They are thick and well built. When the rebel lord declared war on the king, he ordered his soldiers to build wooden hoardings, or temporary passageways, on top of the castle's battlements. Be careful, the castle's defenders can safely attack your troops while hiding in these hoardings.

There is an inner bailey, which is the area inside the castle's walls. This area is also protected by a second set of strong walls and another moat. The garrison of soldiers defending the castle is well trained. Guards patrol the walls and keep a sharp lookout from the towers. The castle also has good supplies of food and livestock.

But the castle also has weak spots. The moat in front of the castle is very narrow and shallow. It could easily be filled in with dirt or have a bridge built over it. There is also a way into the castle from the river through a water gate that is not well guarded. The gatehouse has a wooden drawbridge. You can try to break down the door, or burn it down with your torches.

This castle also has many towers. They are not as strong as regular walls, so you should attack them first. The wooden hoardings along the tops of the walls can also be burned.

Tiled roofs are stronger than wooden ones. Also they cannot easily be set on fire.

Stables where knights' horses are kept

Inner moat

Livestock

Outer bailey

Barns

Round towers are stronger than square ones. They are harder to break down because there are no corners.

Wooden hoardings where defenders hide and drop missiles down onto attackers. They can be damaged by firing lighted arrows onto them.

Roof of the keep is protected by lead. This weatherproofing is also fireproof.

Boats come down the river with supplies and moor at this rear water gate.

Keep

Garden

Inner gatehouse with drawbridge

Inner bailey

Inner walls

The moat is very narrow all around the front of the castle.

Sturdy outer (curtain) walls

Outer gatehouse with drawbridge and portcullis, a heavy wooden or iron gate.

Arrow slits for shooting from a safe position

Before the Siege

Remember, you don't just need brute force to succeed. You'll also need to use your wits to plan the attack and get information. Your tactics should include sending spies into the castle, stopping the castle's food supplies, and blocking enemy troops from coming to the rescue. The more information you can gather about the land, the castle, its lord, and its people, the better.

Hire spies from your own loyal followers if you can. People posing as mercenaries (hired soldiers) make excellent spies because they will be told about the castle's defenses as part of their job. You could also use local merchants or craftsmen who have a good reason to be working inside the castle walls. Things spies can find out include:

1. How many people are in the castle
2. Weak spots in the castle's defenses
3. How large the garrison is
4. How food and water are supplied
5. How ready the castle is for an attack.

If your spies tell you that more troops are on the way to help defend the castle, organize some of your soldiers to ambush them (attack them by surprise). You could also try to capture the lord of the castle. If you succeed, you can hold him until his troops surrender.

Encourage local people, particularly women and children, to enter the castle. They will help use up vital food and water. The defenders are much more likely to surrender if they are hungry and thirsty.

GOOD SPYING TIPS
1. To keep your spies loyal, make sure they are well paid.
2. Brief them carefully, explaining everything, so they understand what they have to do.
3. Train them to use sabotage, like attacking guards or spoiling the water supply.

Your own troops *must* be well supplied. They will fight better on a full stomach. Make contact with merchants and get them to sell you food, clothing, and weapons. You might also need to raid local farms and villages for supplies. It is wise to destroy anything you don't need to prevent any supplies from getting through to the defenders in the castle.

Access to fresh water is very important

Get to know local merchants to make sure you always have supplies

By blocking the river, you can keep supplies from getting to the castle by boat. This can be done by stringing a heavy chain across the narrowest part of the river, just below the water's surface. Boats will crash into this and probably sink. You could also chain logs studded with metal spikes together and float them between the banks. Make sure they are securely tied at each end. Post soldiers on both river banks to defend the barrier.

Defensive screens to protect your archers

Castle keep

Securing logs with heavy chains

Logs are strung across the narrowest part of the river

Logs studded with iron spikes

Post soldiers to defend the barrier

The Soldiers and Their Weapons

How good is your army? The better your soldiers are trained and equipped, the greater your chance of success. Your troops are knights, mounted men-at-arms, footsoldiers, archers, and mercenaries. In addition to your fighters, you will also need cooks, carpenters, smiths, a priest, and a surgeon or two to tend to the sick and wounded. You will also need a good armorer to make, repair, and maintain your armor and weapons. Here are the soldiers that you will have under your command, and their weapons.

Sling-shot | Pike | Glaive | Quilted tunic | Chain mail | Axe

Your footsoldiers will be both ordinary people, made to serve as part of their rent to their lord, and mercenaries. They wear quilted tunics, helmets, and chain mail to protect them when fighting. Their weapons include axes, glaives, slingshots, and maces.

Knights are high-ranking soldiers trained in battle skills and horsemanship since childhood. But they are also expensive to hire!

Mounted men-at-arms | Lance | Crossbow

Mounted men-at-arms are not as high-ranking as knights. They fight on horseback and use lances, bows, swords, and maces. Knights have expensive metal armor to protect themselves and their horses. Poorer men-at-arms might have only chain mail and helmets for protection.

Bodkin   General   Broadhead

Shooting a longbow

Taking aim

"Nocking" arrow onto bow string

Preparing to shoot

Archers are very important. Make sure you have archers using longbows and crossbows. Longbows are as tall as a person. With a longbow, archers can hit their target from over 200 yards away. A good archer can shoot 12 arrows in a minute. Choosing the arrows is important, too. The barbs on a broadhead make it hard to pull out. A bodkin will easily pierce a knight's armor.

Shooting a crossbow

Winding back   Placing bolt   Taking aim

Crossbows use a metal-tipped bolt rather than an arrow. Unlike longbows, you don't need any special training to shoot a crossbow, but they are slower to repeat-fire. A crossbow can be left "cocked." That means the bow is pulled back with the bolt in place, ready to shoot instantly. It is accurate and powerful at short range, but can also shoot long distances.

Glaive: used for stabbing and slashing. Useful against mounted soldiers.

Sword: for slashing and stabbing in close combat

Mace: heavy enough to smash helmets and body armor

Axe: Long pole and sharp, even blade make this an efficient weapon against armor.

Setting Up Camp

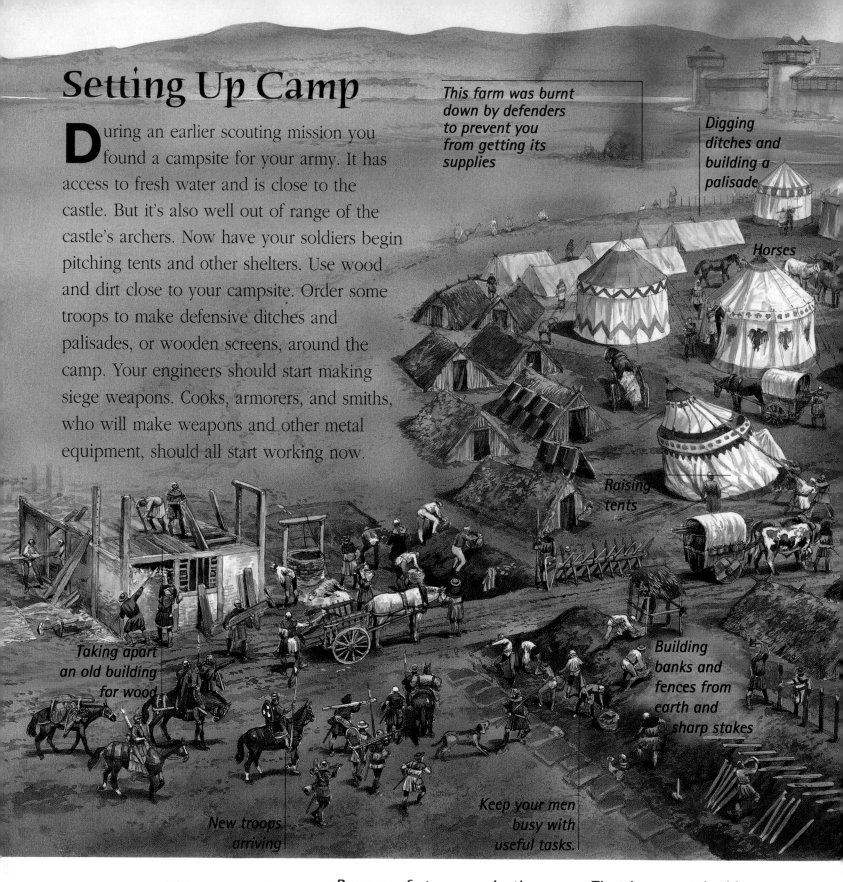

During an earlier scouting mission you found a campsite for your army. It has access to fresh water and is close to the castle. But it's also well out of range of the castle's archers. Now have your soldiers begin pitching tents and other shelters. Use wood and dirt close to your campsite. Order some troops to make defensive ditches and palisades, or wooden screens, around the camp. Your engineers should start making siege weapons. Cooks, armorers, and smiths, who will make weapons and other metal equipment, should all start working now.

This farm was burnt down by defenders to prevent you from getting its supplies

Digging ditches and building a palisade

Horses

Raising tents

Taking apart an old building for wood

Building banks and fences from earth and sharp stakes

New troops arriving

Keep your men busy with useful tasks.

Beware of strangers in the camp. That innocent-looking beggar could be a spy sent by the castle's lord. Warn your soldiers not to talk to anyone too much. They could easily give away information or clues about how or when you are planning to attack. If you think you are dealing with a spy, be careful what you say and watch them closely.

Armed advance party goes toward the castle to make their demands.

Siege weapons

Lookout tower facing castle

Chopping down trees for timber

Livestock

Commander's tent

Commander

Building siege weapons

Practicing fighting techniques

Priests

Armorer

Temporary shelters built from wood and dirt

Butchering meat

Cooks

Fresh water supply

The lord of the castle refuses to give up his rebellion, and will not surrender to your advance party without a fight. Send your herald to announce your attack. If the rebel lord thinks your forces are too great, he might send a messenger back to discuss terms with you. If you're lucky, he might even surrender without a shot being fired.

Castle Defenses

It is important to know what defenses might be used against you, so you can plan ahead and defeat them. The enemy will collect ammunition, such as rocks, to throw at you. They might heat sand and oil over fires to pour on your troops. The garrison will also nail fresh animal hides to the hoardings. This helps make them fireproof.

The garrison will raise the drawbridge to keep anyone from coming in. They will post lookouts so they'll know as soon as you make your first move. They will question, imprison, or even kill anyone they think might be a spy.

If your spies are captured, your plans could be revealed. You might also lose the chance to sabotage the castle from inside.

Animal hides nailed to the wooden hoardings make them fireproof

Hinged wooden shutters between the stone merlons protect archers when they shoot.

The enemy can shoot arrows and pour hot oil or sand onto your troops from "murder holes." These are in the hoarding floor or gatehouse ceiling. Hot sand gets through chinks in the attackers' armor and burns their skin.

Archers have a good view through slits in the walls to shoot your troops. It is almost impossible for you to shoot back through the narrow holes.

Lookout in tower

Defending knight, fully armed

Stone ammunition for hurling

Machicolations

Murder holes

Arrow slit

A captain of the guard questions a castle-dwelling family

Building hoardings

Archer in place at arrow slit

Portcullis

Drawbridge being raised

Spy being jailed

Vaulted (curved) stone ceilings prevent the gatehouses from catching on fire.

Oubliette, a pit for prisoners where they are left to die and forgotten

The Siege Weapons

The goal is to force the castle to surrender. You could do this by starving the enemy into submission, but that takes time. It's much quicker if you can attack with so much force that the enemy cannot resist. Powerful siege weapons will help you get into the castle. These engines are designed to bombard the castle, smashing walls and gates. Then your troops can invade the castle. Be careful, the enemy might have their own siege engines to use against you.

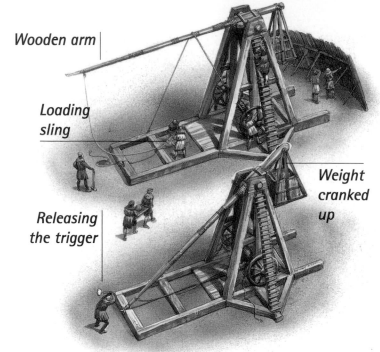

Wooden arm

Loading sling

Releasing the trigger

Weight cranked up

Operating a trebuchet

The trebuchet has a long arm with a heavy weight at one end and a sling at the other. To operate it, load the sling, wind up the weight, and lock it into position. When you release the trigger, the weight drops. This weight drives the arm upward and hurls the missile into the air. Some missiles you can use are dead animals (to spread disease), fire pots, and rocks.

Trebuchet at moment of firing

Sling

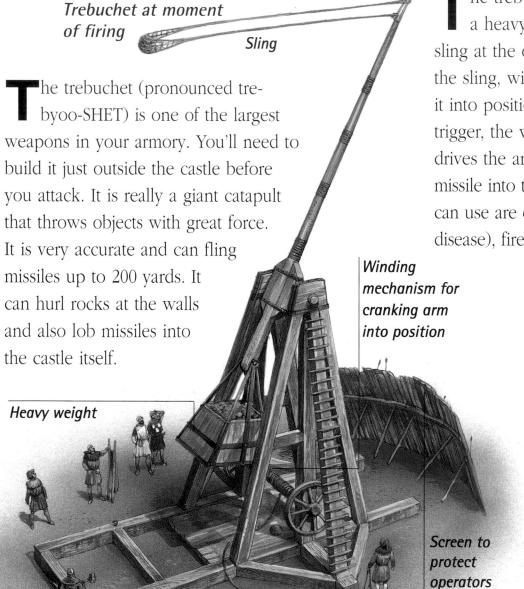

The trebuchet (pronounced tre-byoo-SHET) is one of the largest weapons in your armory. You'll need to build it just outside the castle before you attack. It is really a giant catapult that throws objects with great force. It is very accurate and can fling missiles up to 200 yards. It can hurl rocks at the walls and also lob missiles into the castle itself.

Winding mechanism for cranking arm into position

Heavy weight

Screen to protect operators from arrows

Ammunition for use in trebuchet

Dead animals

Fire pots

Rocks and rubble

The mangonel (pronounced MAN-go-NEL) also catapults missiles, but from a closer range. It is smaller and easier to move than the trebuchet. It consists of an arm and cup mounted on a wooden frame. Its power comes from a tightly wound rope. Just two people are needed to operate the mangonel. One pulls the arm back (which also twists the rope) and locks it in position. The other loads the cup, then releases the arm. The twisted rope springs back and shoots the arm forward. A padded beam stops the arm, but the missile keeps going with great force. The mangonel is very good for smashing walls.

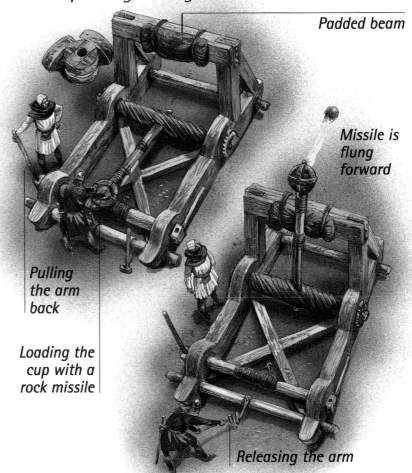

Operating a mangonel

Padded beam

Missile is flung forward

Pulling the arm back

Loading the cup with a rock missile

Releasing the arm

Operating a ballista

One person pulls back the drawstring and locks it into position.

The second man loads the ballista with a large arrow or spear.

The castle's defenders are likely to have their own siege engines. The ballista is the one to watch out for. This is like a giant crossbow. To operate it, pull the drawstring back using a cranked wheel. Then load a large, long arrow, like a spear, onto the bow. Fire it by releasing the drawstring with a lever. The ballista has great aim. You should use ballistas for attacking specific targets, but they won't help with destroying walls.

The first person releases the drawstring with a lever. The bow shoots the arrow with great accuracy.

The Siege Is Underway

The time has come. Negotiations have failed. You must now launch your attack. What methods can you use to storm the castle? Your trebuchet and mangonels can hurl rocks at the walls. If you fill the moat in with rocks and dirt, your soldiers can reach the walls and climb them. You can also place a siege tower outside the high, protected walls. And don't forget the battering ram. Use it to smash the drawbridge door. Protect it from enemy fire with a wooden roof covered in hide.

Crossing the moat and setting up scaling ladders

Archers protected behind wooden mantlets

Filled moat

Trebuchet and rocks for ammunition

Mangonel hurling rocks

Men using slingshots

Bringing water to put out the flames

To protect the soldiers while they fill in the moat, construct a movable penthouse, like a shed on wheels. This carries the materials they need. Wheel it into position wherever the supplies are needed. The wooden roof protects them from arrows. The animal skins on top will also make it fireproof.

Siege tower gives access to the top of the walls.

Defenders try to pull the battering ram out of the way.

Defenders position a mattress to soften the blows of the battering ram.

Filled moat

Defending archer at arrow slit

Load up the penthouse with fascines (bundles of sticks), dirt, and baskets of earth and stones. The soldiers drop the fascines, earth, and stones out of the open front of the penthouse into the moat. This makes a temporary bridge. Finally, they cover the filled-in moat with dirt to stabilize it.

Surviving the Siege

The castle may hold out if it is expecting a relief army to come to its aid. If you suspect this is the case, tell your spies to find out what the defenders are doing to resist your siege. You need information about the castle's military preparations, food supplies, living conditions, health, and morale (well-being).

Spy | Storage barrels | Steward checking stores

ood and dry goods are stored in the basement of the towers. Supplies are carefully checked. If the siege continues, supplies may be rationed, or given out in small portions, to make sure everyone has enough. Your spies should watch the steward while he takes stock of supplies. If they are running low, you need to know about it.

The rebel lord has ordered that all the food in his garden should be harvested and stored. The animals will also need food and water. If food starts to run out, the defenders may decide to kill their livestock for meat. They can dry and salt the meat to preserve it, making it last longer.

Drawing water from well

art of the castle's chapel has been made into an emergency hospital. Priests and women in the castle are taking care of the sick and injured. Sickness has broken out among the people inside. This could be a result of the dead animals your soldiers catapulted over. Morale is low. As the siege continues, the priests offer comfort to the villagers.

Priest | Bandaging wounds | Guard

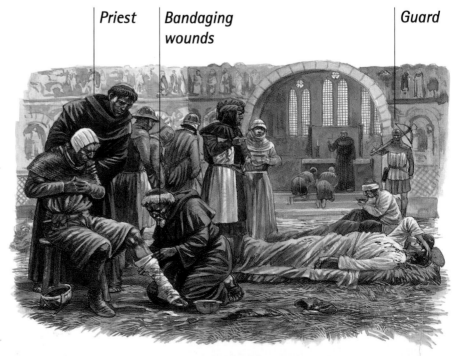

The smith's main task is to make sure all the horses are ready for counterattacks. These smiths are busy making horseshoes and caltrops. Caltrops are four-pronged spikes that always point up, no matter how they fall. When they are scattered on the ground, they injure horses and running soldiers.

Horse ready to have horseshoes put on | Anvil | Caltrops | Blacksmith | Forge

Soldier | Armorer repairing chain mail

The castle's armorers are busy repairing chain mail and armor, sharpening old weapons, and forging new ones in the fire. The lord has ordered that all weapons be inspected and repaired. Making chain mail is hard work that takes a lot of skill. First you make a coil of wire. Next, snip through the wire at the same place along each coil to make several split rings. Then thread each ring through four more rings. Lastly, rivet them closed. The time and effort is worth it because chainmail is lighter and more flexible than armor.

Many villagers moved into the castle for safety when your troops came near. They built makeshift shelters in the outer bailey from wood, cloth, and dirt. It is cold and wet, and there is little food. Soldiers have taken a cart from a villager for wood to build defenses. They cannot last much longer.

Soldiers taking a cart

Makeshift shelters

Cooking

Cloth covering

Making bread

How to Undermine a Tower

The siege is taking too long. Your spies say the enemy is getting ready to counterattack. There might be another army on the way to help the rebel lord. You have to act quickly.

You decide to undermine the South Tower. That means digging a tunnel under it to make it collapse. If the plan works, your troops can overrun the castle.

South Tower

Archer | Fence | Carting away dirt from tunnel | Tunnel entrance

1 The first part of the plan is to dig a tunnel under the tower. You must do this without the enemy suspecting. First, build a fence. The enemy will think this is just a shield for your archers. In fact it will be hiding your miners. Assign workers to cart away the earth and carry the wooden poles.

2 It will take several days to dig below the tower. Make sure you dig far enough beneath the moat. Use wood poles to hold up the sides and ceiling of the tunnel.

Filled in moat

Tower foundations

Diggers at work

Setting up wooden piles

Cross section through ground beneath tower

Tower foundations

Tunnelers escaping the flames

Barrel of tar set on fire

Kindling

3 While your miners are under the tower, they must be very quiet. When the tunnel is finished, place a barrel of tar and some kindling at the base of the stone tower. Then set it on fire and get your miners out as quickly as possible.

4 With a little luck, the fire should burn away those wood support poles in minutes. The roof of the tunnel will fall in. Then the stone walls above it should collapse into the tunnel.

Stone walls collapse

Moat drains into collapsing tunnel

Burning poles give way

This is a long, dangerous operation. The tunnel could collapse or be blown up by the enemy. The moat could flood it. But if all goes well, you will be able to break into the castle very quickly. The tower falling will cause a lot of damage to a large section of the castle wall. The enemy will be taken by surprise. They will probably not have any more men than usual defending that part of the wall. You, on the other hand, can get your forces through the gap in minutes.

This operation must be kept secret. Tell as few people as possible about the plan to keep enemy spies from discovering it.

Your forces entering the castle through a breach in the wall

Crossbow archers giving covering fire

Collapsed front section of tower

Protection against enemy fire

Taking the Castle

If your plan works, the South Tower will collapse and you can take the castle. But don't expect the enemy to give up without a fight. You still have to make it into the inner bailey and find the rebel lord.

The lord and his family will be holed up inside the keep. They will be fiercely guarded by officers. If you make it inside the keep and capture the lord, you then have to decide what to do with your prisoners.

Overpowering enemy guards

Opening the gate

Gate winding gear

Removing wedge so gate can be opened

Castle keep

Drawbridge opened by your soldiers

Your spies can help you break into the well-defended inner bailey. They can overcome the guards and open the gate. Your army can enter the inner bailey and surround the keep.

Fire takes hold of the stable block

Enemy soldiers overwhelmed by your forces

Climbing out of the shaft

Inching up the shaft

Latrine shaft opens onto moat

Keeping guard

Be on the lookout for a hidden or poorly guarded way into the keep.

Your forces stream into the inner bailey

Tower roof damaged by your siege engines

Damaged hoardings

Your soldiers

Look for an unusual way into the keep itself. Latrine shafts or other small openings in the wall are unlikely to be guarded. Once one of your soldiers is inside, have them open a side door to let other troops in. At the same time, send an armed group to the main entrance to attack the garrison there. Then open the final barrier: the gate and drawbridge to the keep itself. You can then find the lord of the castle and demand his surrender.

Lord of the castle

Lord's wife and children

Lord's man-at-arms

At last! You burst into a room where the lord and his family are guarded by only two men-at-arms. He fights hard, but he knows he has lost. Once you've captured them alive, you could accept the lord's surrender and agree on the terms. Report them to the king afterward. The king might imprison or exile the lord. To reward your loyalty, the king might then give you the castle. Victory is yours!

Timeline

Keep castle

Castle styles vary across the world. Originally, though, they all had the same purpose: to provide a stronghold against an enemy. The earliest European castles were called motte-and-baileys. They were little more than wooden forts built on a hill, or motte, next to an enclosure called a bailey. As time went on, the wooden buildings were replaced by stronger stone structures that could protect against fierce attacks. The great age of castles ended when cannons eventually became strong enough to blast through even the thickest of stone walls.

950

Earliest European castle built in Anjou, France.

1000s

Motte-and-bailey castles built in Europe.

1066

Norman Conquest of England. William I builds 87 castles, including square stone towers called donjons or keeps.

1096–1291

The Crusades—wars between Christians and Muslims from 1096 to 1291. Many castles are built by the Christian crusaders to show their military strength and claim the land.

1099

Siege of Jerusalem. The Holy City is taken by the crusaders.

In a motte-and-bailey castle, the motte is a mound topped by a tower. The bailey is an enclosed area beside the motte with houses and barns inside.

1100s

Keep castles are developed. These have extra walls surrounding the keep tower.

1150–1250

Major castle building across Germany.

1200s

Portcullises and rounded towers are introduced into European castles. These were already features of crusader castles.

1272

The crusader castle Krak des Chevaliers in Syria is taken by the Muslims.

Saumur château, France

1337–1453

Hundred Years War in Europe. Active period of castle warfare.

1429

Siege of Orléans. Joan of Arc fends off the English besiegers and wins back the French city.

1567

Siege of Chitor in India. The city is taken by the Moghuls, who attack with cannons.

Neuschwanstein, Germany

1582–1615

Great period of castle building by Samurai knights in Japan. Following the Siege of Osaka in 1615, Shogun Tokugawa Ieyasu defeats the Toytomi clan to secure control of Japan.

1600s

Cannons are now powerful enough to destroy the strongest castle walls. Many castles are ruined or abandoned. Some, such as Saumur château in France, are turned into private homes.

1800s

Castles are built as grand houses, rather than fortresses. The building of Neuschwanstein for Ludwig II, King of Bavaria, Germany, begins in 1869.

Samurai castle, Japan

Glossary

Numerals refer to the illustration below.

arrow slit A narrow opening in a castle wall through which arrows were shot. **See number 1**

bailey An area enclosed by castle walls. **See 2**

ballista A siege engine that is like a giant crossbow.

battering ram A large beam used to break down walls or doors of a castle.

battlements The top of a wall with a series of gaps between raised portions (merlons). **See 3**

caltrops Four-pronged metal stars thrown on the ground to injure horses' and soldiers' feet.

chain mail Flexible armor made up of interlocking metal rings.

crossbow A mechanical bow using short bolts rather than arrows. *See also* ballista, longbow.

curtain wall A wall between two towers. **See 4**

drawbridge A wooden bridge across a ditch or moat in front of a castle gatehouse. Can be raised and lowered. **See 5**

dungeon A prison cell in the basement of a castle. *See also* oubliette.

fascines Bundles of sticks used to fill a moat.

gatehouse A heavily fortified castle entrance. May have a drawbridge and a portcullis. **See 6**

glaive A weapon consisting of a blade on the end of a long pole.

hoardings Wooden gallery attached to the top of a castle wall with holes in the floor, through which defenders attack the enemy.

joust A form of entertainment in which two knights fight on horseback with lances. **See 7**

keep The fortified tower at the center of a castle. **See 8**

keep castle An early style of castle consisting of just the square keep tower.

longbow A large, powerful wooden bow.

mace A metal club used in combat.

machicolations Gaps in the top of a tower or wall for firing missiles onto attackers. **See 9**

mangonel A stone-throwing siege engine.

mantlet A wooden shield on wheels.

masons Skilled workers who build with stone.

merlons The solid parts beween the gaps in battlements. They help protect the castle defenders.

moat A dry or water-filled ditch around a castle. **See 10**

motte-and-bailey An earth mound (motte) with a wood or stone keep next to a courtyard (bailey) surrounded by a fence and ditch.

murder hole An opening in the ceiling through which defenders could fire or drop missiles on the enemy below.

negotiate To talk about demands or terms in order to reach an agreement.

oubliette A pit under the floor for holding prisoners. Reached by a trap-door. **See 11**

palisade A defensive wooden screen or fence.

penthouse A covered cart used to protect attackers filling in a moat.

portcullis A heavy wood and iron protective grill, or pair of grills, inside a gatehouse. It is raised and lowered in grooves by ropes or chains. **See 12**

rampart A stone or earth wall around a castle or camp.

rationing Giving out supplies or food in small portions to make them last longer.

sabotage Deliberate destruction of supplies or plans to weaken an enemy.

siege engine A large weapon, such as a battering ram, trebuchet or mangonel, used to attack a castle. **See 13**

siege tower A wooden tower on wheels, used by attackers to climb over castle walls during a siege. **See 14**

trebuchet A powerful siege engine which works like a large catapult.

undermining Digging beneath the foundations of a building to make it collapse.

Further Reading

Books

Adams, Brian. *Medieval Castles*. North Mankato, Minn.: Stargazer Books, 2007.

Jarrow, Gail. *A Medieval Castle*. Farmington Hills, MI: KidHaven Press, 2004.

Steele, Phillip. *The World of Castles*. New York: Kingfisher, 2005.

Internet Addresses

Ghosts in the Castle!
http://www.nationalgeographic.com/features/97/castles/enter.html

Kids' Castle
http://www.kidsonthenet.com/castle/index.htm

Medieval Siege
http://www.pbs.org/wgbh/nova/lostempires/trebuchet/

Index

A

archer, 9, 10-11, 14-15, 18-19, 22
armor, 10-11, 14, 21
armorer, 10, 12, 21
arrows, 6, 11, 14, 18
arrow slits, 7, 15, 19
axe, 10-11

B

bailey, 6-7, 21, 24, 26
ballista, 17
battering ram, 18-19
battlements, 6
blacksmith see smith

C

caltrops, 21
camp, 12-13
castle, keep, 27
catapult, 16-17, 29
chain mail, 10-11, 21
crossbow, 11, 17
crusader castles, 27
Crusades, 26

D

defenses, castle, 5, 6-7, 8, 14-15
donjon, 26
drawbridge, 5, 6-7, 14-15, 18, 24-25

F

fascines, 19
France, 26-27

G

gatehouse, 6-7, 14-15
Germany, 27
glaive, 10-11

H

herald, 13
hoardings, 6, 14-15, 25
Hundred Years War, 27

J

Japan, 27

K

keep, 9, 24-25
keep castle, 26-27
knight, 5, 10-11, 27
Krak des Chevaliers, 27

L

lance, 10
latrine, 25
longbow, 11

M

mace, 10-11
machicolations, 15
mangonel, 17, 18
mantlet, 18
men-at-arms, 10, 25
mercenaries, 8, 10
merchants, 9
merlon, 14
miners, 22

moat, 5, 6-7, 18-19, 22-23
motte, 26
motte-and-bailey, 26
murder holes, 14-15

N
Neuschwanstein, 27
Norman Conquest, 26

O
oubliette, 15

P
palisades, 12-13
penthouse, 18-19
pike, 10
portcullis, 7, 15, 27
priests, 5, 10, 20

R
rebellion, 4, 13
river, 6-7, 9

S
sabotage, 8, 14
Samurai, 27
Saumur château, 27
scaling ladders, 18
siege, 5, 14-15, 16-17, 18-19, 20-21,
          22-23
siege engines *see* siege weapons
siege tower, 18-20
siege weapons, 12-13, 16-17, 18-19, 25
slingshot, 10, 18
smith, 5, 10, 12, 21

spies, 5, 8, 12, 14-15, 20, 22-23, 24
steward, 20
supplies, 6-7, 8-9, 12, 18, 20

T
towers, 6-7, 22-23, 24, 26-27
trebuchet, 16-17, 18
tunnel, 22-23

U
undermining, 22-23

W
wall, curtain, 7
water gate, 6-7
William I, 26